T0368327

My Life, My Lord, and My Thorn

"A book on love, lust, revelations and, relationship with man and God."

Cecyle Williams

AuthorHouse™
1663 Liberty Drive
Bloomington, IN 47403
www.authorhouse.com
Phone: 833-262-8899

This book is printed on acid-free paper.

All scriptures taken from King James version of the Bible

ISBN: 978-1-6655-0272-6 (sc)
ISBN: 978-1-6655-0273-3 (e)

Library of Congress Control Number: 2020919079

Print information available on the last page.

Published by AuthorHouse 10/06/2021

authorHOUSE®

Preface

After years of writing poems, bible lessons for ministry, articles for magazines and newspapers… My Life, My Lord, and My Thorn stopped being a dream and became a personal goal of mine. After years of not reaching any personal goals, it seems that My Life, My Lord, and My Thorn became a dream deferred and less and less achievable in my eyes. After many years had d and heartache set in I was sure I didn't have the time or the energy to write a book. I needed direction and focus; all of which I did not have. So, after planning, research and much self evaluation that which was only dreamable has now become a manifestation and prayer fulfilled.

Cecyle Williams

My Life, My Lord, and My Thorn is my safe haven that I needed to share with you. You can read and be free in your own emotions, just as I was free in writing mine; embrace the feelings and your thoughts. Release the fear and understand that you are not alone. We live in fear because we never want to pull the covers back. We live in contentment with our lies and hiding behind our fears. You can come the glow of understanding that everything that looks like an issue doesn't have to be. Self awareness and self acceptance belongs to you and you only. Those things that maybe an issue with you, is for God. This isn't your fight. Listen to God speak and give your thorns over to him. He cares for you. You just keep smelling the roses.

About the Author

CECYLE WILLIAMS, Illinois born native; lives, educated, worships, and serves the public in community service on the south side of Chicago.

During Elementary school Cecyle attended a Black History program where she heard a rendition of "Hey Black Child" narrated by Maya Angelou, Cecyle decided to write her first poem, after experiencing rejection and puppy love.

Cecyle, wrote her first article and it was published by The Chicago Defender while she was only in high school, Shortly after Cecyle was asked to join their Jr. Writers Program.

Cecyle lost direction and focus trying to breakthrough on a more professional level writing for teen magazines, that didn't work. She then decided to place her energy more on her children, her relationship with God, and her biblical studies; gaining several certificates for teaching children.

Cecyle Williams

Cecyle received her second try at freelancing when she was given the opportunity to write Sunday School lessons and Bible stories for a publishing company not far from Chicago. After leading a prayer meeting and Bible studies in a transitional home for women where she lived, Cecyle started writing again after having an encounter with death and receiving the vision for this book "My Life, My Lord, My Thorn".

After *years* of struggling with the execution of "My Life, My Lord, My Thorn"... another near death experience got her focused and writing again.

Dedication

To resentment, bitterness, fear, poverty,and unforgiveness generational curses... you have been conquered, no going back; Love still abides in the place where you tried to prosper. You lost again and you always will.

Jadda, Deja, and KeAnne ...I will always love you and will always try to be better for us all.

Table of Contents

My Thorn
Chapter Three

My Life

Chapter One

My Life, a written homage to the people that God has blessed me with. I love my people deeply and wholeheartedly. There is a great reward in people watching, you get to learn people... their needs, trials, victories and triumphs. You get to learn about yourself, how to expand and expound on your own reality. You learn where you can help someone that may be in need. We don't always pay attention to how we can help just by being present in the lives of others. For me being present does not necessarily mean being physically active but it can also mean being emotionally connected. Empaths usually connect easily. Empaths feel feelings and have real emotions that's tied to the lives and stories of others...be it strangers or friends.

I've come across strangers that have bombarded my spirit, family that have taken up space in my mind, lovers that I have surrendered my energy to, and time that I have thrown away. It takes time to learn to appreciate every living being for who they are. Using the process to learn the lesson has been more beneficial than panting over the problems of people. Adoring people from afar has been a pastime of mine that I have enjoyed. It has helped me respect my life and the lives of others. The social destruction that's been going on has affected our emotions, I'm sure. Being secluded has more than likely affected us socially. There are so many disparities. We need each other now more than ever.

Many of these people have touched me very deeply, so much that I could not get them off my mind. A few people have been represented in My Life, my very own children, to the young girl sitting on the gas station post, personal lovers and the souls of babies. I have been emotionally altered by them. It was their life or death that altered me. It's my desire for you to not be in such a rush, that you may see the soul and feel the energy of the people around you. May we all learn to appreciate life a little more.

I hope to inspire others and a lot of you have inspired me
-Tracey Jones

Forgiveness for Growth

Once upon a time I decided to forgive myself for dropping the ball
on me, for not walking in the glow that was designed just for me.
I allowed years and years just to go by,
Without giving my life a real try.
I had no hope and my dreams seemed too far fetched,
it was hard for me to figure out what came next.
I fell short on my decision making.
I rarely gave 100 percent on the chances I was taking.
I listened to people that didn't mean me any good.
I just didn't take the time out for my success as I should.
I smiled on days I should have cried and on the
days I cried I made the choices to hide.
I simply got tired of people expecting perfection from me.
On many days I couldn't even recognize Cecyle.
I got comfortable half living my life and the dependency.
I was trying to experience love and life without living in fear.
But fear was exactly what consumed me with no relief near.
I would say "I was trusting God"and believing
that freedom and liberty was mine.
I would say it with my mouth and not in my heart and mind.
I still wasn't ready to move from that place, space and time.

Having nothing to hold on to or nothing that was mine.
Having no peace,
No place,
No home to call my own.
Everything I'd ever accumulated was all gone.

So for that I had to forgive myself.
I also had to learn to forgive some of you.
I heard some of what you said and your melancholy words stuck like glue.
Because of your unkind words many times I turned to my own vices,
Those were the days and nights I wasn't the nicest...
days didn't come home,
I shopped and focused on retail therapy.
I ate the wrong foods knowing I had not one but six tumors inside of me.
I fell into the darkest parts of my mind, not paying
any attention to the wasted time.
Still not giving myself a chance, waiting for someone
to accept me and clap their hands.
Not once did I think of me.
I lost good years waiting on many of you to love me.
As pathetic as it may sound...many of you kicked me when I was down.
So, as I forgive myself and I forgive many of you too because
I don't look like half the stuff I've been through.

Cecyle Williams

Most High God, please forgive me for not being accountable for
the life and gifts inside of me, for allowing the opinions of others
pierce my destiny, and letting depression steal from me, for not using
wisdom in my own life, although I know some may never get it right.
I'm now in full understanding that's not what I want for my life.
I will walk in the good of the day and covered in your light.
I forgive those who hated me secretly,
They had no idea I was fighting to be happy.
They had no idea of the times I was turned around,
They had no idea how life had me bogged down.
So all powerful merciful and gracious God hear my cry speak to
every soul, dry every teary eye, mend each and every broken heart.
give to those that need a fresh start.
Breathe the breath of life into me and all of these your people,
let us show your love God, in all that we do.

I've sat and watched you kill. (**A Leave of Absence**)

You've killed our Fathers and Sons, our Cousins, Aunts and Uncles, Our Sisters and Mothers and I shudder.

I shudder to think what you would do to me if no one was looking, because even with your camera vest on people are still getting mistaken, bodies are still being tooken, voices are not heard,and people still misunderstood their lives are being forsaken.

But you're crying out."I wanna go home at the end of the day", but you took a life that could have been spared and you never cared. This is NOT kill or be killed, There has to be a better way.

So, exactly... what makes you more worthy to make it home over me today?

Why do you get to see your family... but my family can't see me?

What makes you think you are too good to die on these streets... Along with the people that look like me?

What makes you so special that when you cry out "I can't breathe" how in the hell your lungs receive air before anybody? Why can't I wear a hood and question your authority?

Why are your answers filled with hate and smug responses from your insecurities?

Look if you don't have answers to my questions..don't just shoot me in my back.

Black people should go home too and I'm just simply stating some facts.

You wanna be fair,learn your job. You want someone to care, first, have a heart.

You don't feel secure get some fucking therapy.

Don't come to work and relieve your stress...by putting 12 shots in a black man's chest.

Some shit is just easy to do, like listen when we say please don't shoot.

We have enough to worry about.

Our children are being bullied and beaten.

Our sisters are gone missing. People riding the wave until we vote, I'm talking about the politicians.

There are people living outside that don't have coats, food,or love.

Yet, you walk around thinking you are the law over and above...we should feel protected and served.

You're no pillar to our communities, you can't even keep it safe.

You are more of a problem than a solution who in the hell gets locked up then raped... or worse dies in holding some don't even get to catch the case.

If you focus on THE JOB more, less people will get carried away, and

If you are afraid you won't make it home, then take a leave of absence... WITHOUT PAY!

Beautiful Black Golden Girl

Beautiful Black Golden Girl, you are full of beauty and of light. You don't have to ever worry, you won't miss one thing that's meant for your life. You are the very thing that has designed this earth, and it's been your inheritance since your birth.

Beautiful Black Golden Girl, it's nothing European, Asian, South or North American about you, Nothing Australian or Artic about your pearls of truth. There's a thousand years of wisdom in your curls, coils of oil that runs through your veins, rays of sunlight bend when the Son speak your name. So what makes you think Hells demons don't do the same. Your very presence is like a cleansing rain. Your very presence is as deep as the Ocean floor. Your very presence reaches the galaxies and far more. Your very presence shakes your haters core, but when you're not around they need you to teach them Moor, your people all the Moor. To teach the evolution of life, and rebirth just as before, just as always, just as now, just as never the same again, just as every fingerprint and every footprint in the sand.

This Revolution will not be televised, something cosmic happens when the Moonlight hits your skin... it needs to be seen with bare eyes, people are drawn in.

Beautiful Black Golden Girl, you are worth your weight in gold. Your Creation is the greatest love story ever told. Penned, by God himself, and a King bound paged and words that start with "In the beginning" the hottest lyrics ever spoken. Tales of victories, and the overcoming; not designed with one flaw or any shortcomings . Excuse me? Miss, your rivers are running. There are people with their rafts, riding your waves of the rivers of your truth, they realize your shine and want to be just like you, stand next to you, glow like you, rock that skin and afro like you do, but they are nothing like you, and they know it too, so don't be a shame to flow like you do.

Beautiful Black Golden Girl, If you don't know who you are, who you really really are, don't ask anybody, look to the heavens and the stars.

Beautiful Black Golden Girl, you are the nucleus of my world. You are what has been, what is, and what shall be. You are generations of Queendoms and genealogy. You are Magical DNA, you are the unicorns and pyramids of today. You are the Diamond mines of untouch melanin. Your eyes hold the souls of those once living. You hold the rhythm of life in your belly. You nurse Nature and gracefully turn water into wine when you bathe. Flowers spring up from the souls of the dead when your love is made. You are unable to throw shade. You throw wisdom and guidance. You break the necks of those in defiance. You are an everlasting being your energy is never-ending. You are all the colors of the rainbow, that's more than enough. You are enough.

Beautiful Black Golden girl

Simple & *Sweet*

It's so easy to allow what's wrong with us die, when you smile at me with that twinkle in your eye.

So *Simple* to drift into a trans, when you are kissing my lip and taking off my pants.

No, it's not complicated at all, to forget those disrupting calls.

So *Sweet* to smell your presence... and not have to dream.

To be sure that the bond it's just felt and also seen.

So *Simple* to allow two minds to sync, for you to feel me when I over think.

So kind of you to love my pain away and to let my body come out to play.

So *Sweet* to taste you and the pleasure you have to give. So Sweet to taste the life you live.

So *Simple* to lay, indulge, inspire, and spark a fire.

Cecyle Williams

So easy to watch us burn, blaze, smolder, to desire, to entice, to beguile, to hypnotize, to get higher.

Simple & *Sweet* to see you and all your flaws. To live and love in spite of them all.

ASIA'S CROWN

My crown is round, and my crown is thick,
It doesn't just hold jewels...it also holds a pics.
It should not be kept in a museum or in a case,
because my crown is loud, it has volume and base.
There is no containment, the style is wild,
That doesn't mean I'm an animal, it means I'm not your child.
So since there are no kids around...let's get this understanding.
All roots don't come from the ground.
This afro was birth with DNA from careful planning.
Majestic strands of beauty sweet like candy.
The fullness of life can overwhelm many
and it can also get your fingers crushed.
So be aware, you can look but PLEASE DON'T TOUCH.
The defiance of gravity and elevated truth,
your comb can't handle this hair...it's at a hunnit proof.
It's not watered down nor is it chemically tamed.
I'm not killing myself to get denounced by my ancestors dishonored with guilt
and shame. You're both offended and impressed by my hair that is 4C because
you don't know how coils of love can come from hair this Nappy.

Bed of Lies

You can tell me anything,
I'll sit in your face and listen to it all.
Tell me that the sky is purple and it's about to fall.
Tell me that the world is flat and it's never been round.
Tell me you can take me to the moon,
when I know I've never left the ground.
Tell me there is spot on a zebra and stripes on a cow,
tell me anything and I will never question how.
Tell me yes when all I see is no.
Tell me what I want to hear, and only what I need to know.
Make your lies taste sweet and easy to swallow.
Then I can pretend your brain isn't shallow,
your heart isn't that hollow and you've been trying to play
me since the first hello.
So in your bed of lies I can freely wallow.

Text Message

B my muse, B the reason Y my wrds fuse.
...Trth is here is whr I wnt U2B.
If Im UR purpose, then B my dstny.
I put my hrt&soul on the line.
&If I lose, then U lose,
I have 2 Utlze this time.
U a gamblin' man,
U play wit winnin'on UR mind.
But if U push me away.
whats the pnt of tryn'
Ily,&
Idk if w/U is whr I shld B.
U want me 2 trst U,
But U cnt and wnt trst me.
I wnt 2 udrstnd, if U will tlk 2 Me.
Tell Me of UR hrts&pains
So I may luv U cmpltly.
I can luv U in spite of UR faults
& not bcuz of my needs.
I can say it a 1000X but,
that wnt make U have faith N'Us
or bliev me.
U've been hurt, Ive been hurt2.
I wont be bullied N2 given up onU.
N relationships there's reciprocity.
Its the give&take to rmnd Uof how thngs shld B.
Im no tryn'2 hrt orB hrt NE more N at this
pnt its been more than I bargained4.

Toxicity

For every positive there is an equal and opposite negative. For every Yin there a Yang, for the Ups there are Downs, There are glass half full and glass half empty types. There are tons of people that maneuver and live on lower frequencies. Unfortunately they are stuck in the past, living in shame, guilt, and embarrassment. They chose to keep company with those on lower levels because it's familiar. The "crabs in the barrel" concept is perfectly depicted as being stuck with others in a bad situation fighting to get out and someone beneath you pulls you down continuously. More negatives arise as people are forced to live in their pain. Some are neglected and forced to go to bed hungry and wake up the same, forced to sleep on the streets, forced to live subjected to this lawless world, forced to be gentrified and colonized, forced to die, force to care when they need to cry...so someone else can live comfortably in their lie.

As flabbergasted and dumbfounded as I am, it tickled me to see the dangers and traps that are set before me, Cancer causing elements in everything I do, Like, our clothes, intimate products and yes even my food. Yes, our food, before it reaches the market it's already pumped with lies, meats are soaked and colored with harmful agents, a seemingly effective disguise.

We are shackled to the history that's been designed for you and me. We are given the lesser piece of the American Pie, a pie that wouldn't exist without slavery slaves that worked, created and invented and 85% of everything that we utilize. There is a 100 degrees of falsehood and savatree. Broken and bitterness in hearts of people that we see and people in neighborhoods making it…barely, governed neighborhoods not giving a damn but living lavishly. The capitol dining on debauchery. I'm the bane of lady liberty existence with ignorance as proof of white supremacy.

There is levels to this toxicity

Words like civil and inclusion don't sit well with me. Do you expect me to accept a civil law from people that's never been civil to people who look like me.

Becoming.

transcend this moment in time with me. We can go into our future and fulfill our destiny, re-live our past and recreate our right now. Reside inside my mind and slow me down. Let's touch the heavens together and together defeat our hell. I'll become a flower and you become a bee, fly in on a warm summer day and pollinate me. Be my wise King and my vaillant stable boy let me throw myself at your feet. I'll be a mighty oak, you can be a lover's hug come and save me. Let our energies sync. Bluetooth our vibrations and design a masterpiece. Paint the ceilings of my mind so men can gawk and gape from behind a redline. Leave this shell of a body and become a celestial being holding all cosmic power; energy, space, and time. We can become alternative universes you and I, like algorithms of the mind an infiniti math solutions of 3.14

Moments in time

When self confidence touches consciousness
they date and become intertwined.
That's when spirits are calculated by dimensions and
I became aware of existence...yours and mine.
Our greatest delusion became the concept of time.
Opportunities are birthed by energy, they are the
love child of action aligned with positivity.
Beautifully pictured purpose is defined.
I manifest my reality.
I draw what I need, it comes through me.
I just created my destiny.
The beauty of spirit is that it knows no time,
At any point in life you can hit reset, pause, or rewind.
It's evident our bodies reproduce what we need the most.
It's how it heals itself, it's how life grow.
It's how positive words and energy multiply extra days to our life.
It's how we find soulmates when the mind and vibes are right.
Spirit instructs time and dictates positive thoughts and a focused mind.
It's Elevated Energy and the Great Divine.

Petals, Stems, and Thorns

I have forgotten the sound of the rain as it falls on your petals
as the mist hits my ear.

It pains my chest to know that you are no longer here.

I still grieve you even though your body left this world
long ago.

The beauty of your petals remains in vases that you birth and
left here to grow.

So, we are surviving merely by the grace of God and the
memories left behind.

If we gave our souls to be with you, it still would not buy us
enough time.

and, If it meant that the sun would shine on you one more day,

I would gladly breathe my last breath and then give the rest
away.

There are stems here trying so hard to push through new little
buds.

What they need right now is you.

Your watering soul and a lot more your hugs, to nourish our
baby rosebuds

They need to know how to gracefully drink the shine from the sun.

And, how to shelter themselves when the storms come.

Your stems are bending but not broken,

They need your encouragement, your presence, and your advice softly spoken.

It's hard telling someone to be of good cheer, when they are living their absolute worst fear.

letting them know that everything will be alright,

New mercies come with new daylight.

When there is no one they can trust in sight.

We are living our biggest fight.

Yet with my thorns you still loved me.

I was strengthened because of your love for me.

Even if I accidently prick my flesh,

you loved me in the center of all my mess.

You embedded in me qualities that forces me to be like you

Everyday I aspire for those qualities to shine through.

Love you Mommy
Helen Rose Williams

My Lord

Chapter Two

My Lord chapter speaks to the more spiritual side of myself. My Lord are revelations I come to understand, spiritual evolutions I have experienced, songs (maybe) and poems. It is the God in me and the very presence of God in my life. It's the nucleus of who I am and why I am Soul, Spirit, and Energy. Also, My Lord is a compilation of writings based on what God has given me, what I have studied and learned . One thing I know for sure...God never gives revelation to one without giving confirmation that follows. Just when you think you are not certain God will send a messenger of confirmation. As I was writing this book I had 2 other books brewing inside of me. I was conflicted not knowing which book to continue with. The encouragement of others gave me the security that I needed to know I am writing the correct book for the right time.

My Lord had many confirmations for me. I expected to feel a move of God as I wrote. As I wrote, I expected to see the face of God in the people I was writing about. Not only that, the evolution of self became inevitable. There was no way I could stay blinded by traditional teaching and it's uncertainties, when there was so much God to experience in my life. My Lord had such an uprising in my spirit my natural man became lighter. I took God out of the box.

God has given us many avenues to reach the mental state of peace. The practice of prayer and meditation brings forth vision and vision birth manifestation. I had to learn to love God for enlightenment and allowing me to become a light source. It is truly a blessing to tell all of you it is so much more God than we know because we put Spirit in a box. God is in the winds and the waves, in the trees and sun, in the moon and the stars. God is all around us and our beloved that has transitioned is all around us. Everything that is and has been, will always be. We cannot have this without our creator. It was a blessing in writing My Lord. You will be blessed to write your story as well.

The g

Law vs. Love

LAW

We know that Religion is based on laws and condemnation. Question, Are we bound by law? The very laws that are given to us, keeps us restricted from liberty and free will. We are more subjected to fail and miss our mark because of so many laws that are commanded for us.

Contrary to popular belief following laws don't and will never make you a good person. Following the law only makes you controlled and law abiding. Law abiding makes good for religion and/or a productive citizen. Laws and regulations are developed to apply a mandate and to distinguish order. Where there is law there is a hierarchy. Mankind, far too often, reject law for self-will. It is self-will that dictates and establishes who we are, it is the structure of our character and is the epitome of our desires. Self-will tells us if we should follow the law or break it.

Matthew 5:17
Think not that I am come to destroy the law, or the prophets: I am not come to destroy, but to fulfil.

LOVE

To define love I would have to explain intimacy. Love is a bond instead of bondage. Love is established through some form of creation or development. People usually love what they are often drawn to and/or attracted to. Love has an element of servitude. Where there is love, the fruit of the spirit are not too far away. Conversation and communication is a great way to start a relationship. Having a purpose for a relationship and being intentional in that relationship builds the relationship. There are very few deal breakers and restrictions when you have real love. No one is perfect, love is forgiveness in my eyes. When love is applied your flaws are not as large as you think. When love is applied so is grace and mercy. There are 3 possibly 4 different definitions of love...and still, the greatest act of love is sacrifice.

John 3:16
For God so loved the world, that he gave his only begotten Son, that whosoever believeth in him should not perish, but have everlasting life.

A Prayer for the use to be's

God this is my prayer for the ex's that we all once were, we've all been something, and ex someone.
Some of us are still in it and some of us are running.

No, things are not what I thought...
and yes, I lost some of those battles I fought.
I even lost some friends along the way but I'm grateful for the ones that decided to stay.
Give them peace inside of their heart, let them know that you are still God.
Protect them as this world turns cold, and bless their home and all that it may hold.
Give them the happiness that being a Child of God brings. Help release the guilt, it only hinders things.
Restore, Rejuvenate and Renew, so that we may learn to love like you.
Convict, Constrain, and Contempt all negativity, so that we may learn the lessons and live happily.
Let our light so shine in the lives of others, so we can be of love to our sisters and brothers.

Grace and Mercy

I've struggled with why you love me...I don't deserve the love you've shown me.
surely I haven't done much of what you asked or said.

At times I get inside my own head, and start to think am I better off dead . I remember that's not what the word said.

When I'm not fit to live or allow to die. My guilt tells me "you can't be saved, so why try". The purpose in me starts to cry, I can feel it say, "I shall live and not die."

That's when your grace covers my failures and your mercy covers my tries, Your love covers all my sins and my silent cries.

It covers me on weary days . It covers me in my human ways. It covers me during my test. It covers me when I'm not at my best.

That's when your grace covers my failures and your mercy covers my tries, your love covers all my sins and my silent cries.

Cecyle Williams

Why you love me so, I may never know why. Why you reached back to saved me on Calvary, why you hung bled and died, I may never know why

But that's when your grace covers my failures and your mercy covers my tries and your love covers all my sins and my silent cries.

My "No" Season

We often forget to thank God for what he has saved us from. We don't thank him for the things he has denied us and certainly not for the dangers we don't see. We are not aware of the obstacles we miss everyday, so there is no point to bring them up to God in our prayers (so we think). When the thing that we desire will enrich us greatly comes into view but it doesn't come through; we seldom forget to thank God for protecting us. A delay isn't a denial. When do we get to the point in our lives the blessing is in the trying and the process is the testimony, and the testimony is what makes us strong. We rarely revere God for keeping us with closed doors. How do you love God in your season of No!

Sorry Ms.Williams, The loan wasn't approved. No, Ms.Williams your application wasn't accepted. Ms. Williams we can't ok your offer, Ms.Williams you need a bigger down payment, No, Kids or pets are allowed Ms.Williams. What do you do with so much rejection? When you are doing all that you know to do. Align yourself with God and the word. You are waiting for one yes and all you hear is no. You've entered into the season of No! Trust your process. Don't allow your peace to be the payment.

John 15:7

If you abide in me, and my word abides in you, ask for whatever you wish, and it will be done for you.

We as Christians like the part of Jesus being our saviour, saving us from sin damnation and Hell's fire. Oh the Church go into a praise when the preacher is talking about how Jesus died to save us from sin, how we send up a praise when we are on the saved side of of trial and tribulation, and ohhhh how he has kept me from death physically and spiritually dangers toils and snares. He has kept me from my enemies even when the enemy was me, and evils of which I was not aware. God has kept me.

Romans 8:29

We know all things work together for the good of them that love GOD, To them that are called according to his purpose.

Thank GOD!!!! for every denial, rejection, closed doors and cancelled assignment. You know better than I. I give you praise, glory and honor. In Jesus name Amen

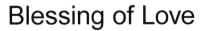

Blessing of Love

Blessings of love, my Redeemer
Blessings of love, my Provider
Blessings of love, my Strong Tower
Blessings of love, my Shield
Blessings of love, my Healer

Blessings of love you give to me,
heavenly angels watch over me
when trouble falls on every side,
In your protection is where I'll hide.
I've made your heart my resting place
Consuming fire burns this place.

You are my Redeemer, My Strongtower, and my Shield.
In my storm you provide and heal.
In the middle of my storm I've found my faith.
Be my guide and saving grace

I'm grateful that your love has kept me.
Your blessings rain down on me.
They are everlasting
You are faithful to me when you don't have to be.
I don't deserve your love

Cecyle Williams

Blessings of love, my Redeemer
Blessings of love, my Provider
Blessings of love, my Strong Tower
Blessings of love, my Shield
Blessings of love, my Healer

Out from the norm

Withdrawn from my norm, I questioned my faith.
I sought out the truth surrounded by Christians hate.
Withdrawn from my norm an unexpected journey to seek the
face of Jesus amongst the presence of men.
So I tallied up all of their truth.
I saw what was evident to piece together what is still relevant.
I've spent years in service and more trying to be perfect.
Now I'm s any of this been worth it?
I've learned countless as hymns... only to find out that some
were written by slave masters who raped and killed Black
Women and Men.
Feeling a deep guilt there were tears that I cried, struggling with
how hard I tried.
Making sure I've learned the difference between reverence and
fear,
Preparing for the rapture because the end time is always drawing
near.
I've prayed many nights that my change would come,
only to find out that time waits for no one.
As I further my studies and my heart began to break, what
followed is what most worried me today.
I asked myself could all this be true?

Have the people I've trusted to teach me been betraying me too?

So was Adam and Eve the first created or not?

Who exactly was the wife of Lot?

So, you said Jesus was there when God created me too.

When God said in OUR image and likeness, JESUS was in the room ?

What am I supposed to do with this information, it's all so new?

Nobody told me this and I've gotten so confused.

Since I've been on this journey, looking at people strange.

I'm wondering how our people are going through life without any change?

How are we not searching for more of what is the truth and still living more of the same?

Like why are we believing this Southern Baptist teaching and where is the proof in which it pertains?

Isn't that what the Bible tells us to do?

To study to show ourselves approved.

Speaking of the Bible…

That's something else I have to admit.. I need help concerning it.

I'm questioning everything.

I've stepped into a matrix.

Who is Jesus?

Did he look like me?

What is his connection to my African ancestry?

Why does it have to be such a mystery?
It has been said we are not supposed to question God but to have faith.
How can we not question faith when Christians carry so much hate?
How can you tell me to turn the other cheek, when it was a Southern Baptist that continues to oppress me.
How many kill the spirit in .
It's a Christian that sits in the highest office to make this country racist again.
I don't that Jesus is real, honestly I don't know his name.
What I oppose is...Christianity being taught out of hate and because of self hate it's still being taught the same.

In My Vein

Philippians 4:13 Affirmation

I was made for such a time as this.
No demon on this earth can stop me.
There's no Devil in Hell that can hold me.
No situation can block me.
I was created to Shine.

Nothing is impossible,
all things are obtainable,
Nothing is unreachable,
I am capable
With a God whose unmeasurable

With faith, I believe it
With plans, I see it
With work, I change it
If I try, I can make it
And with God its possible

I can do all things, all things through Christ...Christ that Strengthens me.

Hey God?

I think I met my husband today. Hey? Hey God, are you listening to me?

I think I met my husband and ohhhhh is he a vision to see,
but I'm certain you know him better than me.
My husband's wisdom and love is unparalleled, it goes unmatched.
He has an aura about himself that screams humanity.
He... has had everyone's back.
He is a teacher and a lover.
His strength is my peace,
I'll never have to question his fidelity his honesty will prove me.
He is a joy to be with.
His laugh and smile is everything,
it's authentic and genuine, the pleasure that the sound brings me.
I tried to consume every ounce of him before time devoured me.
He calms my insecurities, and engaged in my uncertainties,
he is complicated and simple as ABC's and 123's.
He is smart but not arrogant, confident for sure.

Flirtatious but not annoying, easily the remedy to the dis ease of loneliness,

he is my cure.

Musically he's 3 dope verses and a hook on a jazz track, with a sample of Amazing Grace playing in the back.

Logical, Critical, still Nonjudgmental, Personal and very Intentional.

Analytical and yes even at times Lackadaisical,

but that rejuvenates his mind, body and soul. I can't wait to enjoy him and become the love that gears and powers it all.

I can't wait to be his partner in love and crime.

I can't wait to save, secure and sanctify.

I can't wait to solidify, seal and submit.

Now that I see what a husband is I can't wait to commit.

God, I believe I met my husband today.

I just don't know if he met his wife the same way.

Black Woman

Taste every desire playing in my head.
Cater to every need between my legs.
Free me from this anticipation and make love to me beyond my imagination.
I will rise up and deliver to you the Queen that is inside of me, and that doesn't start or stop with my sexuality.
You say when and I'll give you a love deeper than the horizon.
Tighter than the vice grips on your Schwinn.
Wetter than the tears that I cried in the beginning, and more real than the truth that is hidden.

I can bring laughter to your heart like a 90's sitcom.
Make you feel like a man once you pull me close into your arms.
Make you feel love like you never knew or ever known, a love like you've never been giving, a love like you've never been shown.
You'll wake up every morning embracing the God given gift of life;
Mad cause you gotta go to sleep not wanting to miss a second of this new life.
The real love of a good Black Woman will get your life right.
Get you a Black Woman, she will change your life.

GOD IS

The Love of God is found inside of us.
God's love is literally found all around us.
If you look in the face of a baby you can see it in their eyes and their smile.
You can see the face of God when you look at a child.
If you stand still you can feel God in the breeze,
you can hear God speak as the wind blow through the trees,
You can see him move when the leaves change color...
change in nature is God and nature is itself the mother, what is manifested from the two are sisters and brothers.
With the rays from the sun you can feel God's energy,
The heat you experience is the Sun of God's majesty.
You can feel God cleansing you in the rain, drops of love on your face freeing you to smile again.
A sunset hiding behind city buildings,
the beauty of a sunrise in the distance both are signs of God's presence.
In a field of flowers you can smell God presence too,
You can feel him on petals like morning dew.
God is the galaxy, the stars, and the moon that sits so high.
He is the very colors of the rainbow that decorate the sky.
God is celestial energy just like you and I

My Thorn

Chapter Three

My Thorn chapter is exactly what you think it is. There may be a few questions as to why I would combine this explicit style of writing in this book, How did I come to express my sexual desire in this way and also, why was it important for me not to make a separate book just for this chapter. The answer is simple, I am a true believer that our creator designs us perfectly, but because of the knowledge of good and evil we now have flaws. Our flaws we need to give to a higher power everyday. I would not dare try to exclude my personal flaws that keep me praying and in the face of God . My Thorns are X-rated, lustful, prideful, selfish and have hindered me from personal growth over the years. My Thorns are proof that many times I have failed myself and others; and many times I had to start over. I have to seek God for My Thorns and my desires. My Thorns are also the reason why I have had 4 children (that have changed the life of someone). While I was looking for a physical love in man I found a spiritual love that only God can fill.

I don't wish to fabricate the truth about our thorns but be completely honest about them by accepting who we are without glorifying them. Your thorns may not be like mine or coincidentally your thorns could be exactly like mine. We all have to learn to address our mess and unpack our issues. We can start the process by not placing blame and admitting exactly what thorns we have in our lives. Understand I'm not saying celebrate them or allow them to run wild in my spirit or my physical body, but I acknowledge them and control them. If you lack the ability to manage your thorns, just know that God's grace is sufficient for us all. I have suffered in my turmoil long enough to encourage you. I've experienced enough hell in my life to tell you that you don't have to be perfect. These pre-dated social guidelines are no longer adequate. The only rule we have is to love each other. So, It doesn't matter which thorn you are struggling with, they all belong to God.

The Vulgarity of My Thorns is what causes confusion and it has also stirred up passion inside of me. The thorns in my life have inspired real love and unconditional love. My Thorns have caused me heartbreak and pain. People have tried to make me ashamed of some decisions I have made and I just refuse to be. I am neither ashamed nor will I be shamed. God has made me with these thorns and I'm going to live with them until I grow past them or heal from them. Despite all of it, know that your test becomes your testimony.

Unapologetically Me

Music and Dance

To the bass of your lips and the beat of your heart, the rhythm of your touch you make me wanna sing. Sing to your hip hop style, ole skool mentality, jazz demeanor, and neo soul and classical ways. You make me wanna sing, But... I won't.

You speak, you speak to me in volumes. You are my equalizer, when I am off and unbalanced, I am at my best when I hear your sound. Together we create a bangn' groove that our friends can flow to. You make me wanna sing but I can't. What I can do is hit your buttons and turn you on. Push our equipment up and against my walls and dance!

Yeah, that's what I can do...dance to the tune that is you. The same tune jammin to since the sixth grade. I'll do leaps and lifts to your symphony. I can 2 step to your gospel, slow grind to your blues, sway to your swing. You are the soundtrack to my life. You spin me.

CHEMISTRY

I looked inside your soul and found my peace, not only did I find what I have never seen, but you WANTED to give to me. We rushed into moments that were stimulating dialects on the rights and wrongs, rhythms and rhymes, space, order, dimensions and time. The things I thought were crazy you seem to think they were fine. If I thought to tell a person cell rebirth and rebuilding starts with your mind, people would look at me funny and say stay quiet and just keep still; all the time thinking...It seems as if she's taken the red pill. I soaked up your energy from your smile and your laughter, meanwhile thinking of our nappily ever after. Totally separated the ones from the twos. Falling for the process of chemistry, because that's what theoretical scientists do. We deal in the shoulda woulda coulda and the what if's, constantly unraveling the entanglements of the shallow truth. Like masterminding a puzzle then taking it apart, just to put it back together again purposely making it heart. Me, a Theoretical Scientist and You, a Social Chemist evidence of emotional bliss. My newest study: you, me on spiritual enlightenment and social distancing.

Interstate 90 me please

Hands on the steering wheel, his eyes on the street. I'm feeling some kinda way with him smiling at me. There's a few miles behind us with several more to go. So I plant myself firmly in my seat enjoying the scenery as we go, I'm thinking this joy ride will be a much needed treat. So I brace myself for what could be... a very awkward ride, but it wasn't to my surprise. With my emotions running high and my body trembling out of control, I'm trying to explain to myself just how this could go. As I try to pretend his presence wasn't a factor, I tried to cover my nerves by putting on headphones and it still didn't matter. I'm going to put my body under submission. So I throw myself and the chair in a relaxed position. He turns on the radio and starts to sing, I act as if I'm not listening. So, now my mind has cultivated some naughty things. I'm trying to see what these next few miles will bring. I pushed back my seat and kicked shoes out the way, I had my easy access clothing on... I kinda planned it that way. He runs his hands up my thighs. so I grabbed his wrist and just closed my eyes. So I played coy, all that fresh air was good to breathe. I named that experience " Interstate 90 me please".

My 2nd Soul

a separate entity and spiritual being wrapped up in masculinity. a brave heart and caring mind, giver and generator of time. Master of compassion, sender of light, Vision maker and deliverer of sight.

Teaching me to speak life into myself and the negative vibes subside. You partnered my inner peace with the unconditional love I have inside. You've talked me off my emotional ledge, as I teetertotted in and out of the destructive places in my head.

I want to feel you grow inside of me. Feel your energy consume me. Bringing light to darkness, like a healing rain. Soak me with your sunshine, and drain the pain. Cover my ego and humble my anger. Let me lay before your wisdom and feast upon my favor. Stretch my thoughts and watch my pride die. I'll give you all of me and you know why.

You know what to do with my insecurities
You know what to do with my fears
You know what to do with my flaws
and being the man that you are, you knew how to handle them all.

Questions?

Do your fingers want to taste my skin?
Are you pressed to feel me deep within?
Did my body tell you I would never say no?
Did I hear your heart say,
"again". But I'm not ready tho ?
Was it how I walked your way telling you it was a go?
Did the look in my eye tell you I wanted more?
Did you think you would ever hear me say close the door?
Did you imagine my shirt off and
pants on the floor?
See, you've already shown me what you've been waiting for? Now tell me, how can I serve
you more? Become your desire and all that you have hoped for.
Your peace, your tranquility, your grace and safe space.
Be the love you need to put a smile on your face.
No worries or race, just a natural pace.
I'm more worried about our faith, and all this will take.
Let's make some dates. tell our friends to start saving dates.
Who said lust can't open doors.
ask God to reveal and he'll give you all you've been asking for unconditionally love and a
lot more.

Redefining Me!

I want to become better for you!

I want to stop doing things I use to.

Get up and out of old nature.

Not just become the greatest but I know I can be even greater.

Rise above stereotypes and mediocrity.

Present to you a better version of Me.

Be the woman of your dreams.

No Nagging, No more fighting and cussing,

Redefine myself for a more perfected King,

Celebrate you, your efforts,

and whatever they may bring.

Appreciate you for the little things.

To Love you,

allow your weaknesses to become what makes you strong.

Cecyle Williams

Your ways may be different but that doesn't mean you have to be wrong.

I want to feed on your intellect and explore your mind.

Drift slowly through your thoughts,

without bombarding you with mine.

I won't run your you past in your face,

but show some trust in its place.

I did not say it would be easy but I will keep trying.

I will do anything to show the culture....no more dividing.

We can love each other unconditionally,

Your battle is with the world,
it's not with me.

No more manipulation, only love and security.

Peace and purity.

Give me a better you and I'll give you a better me.

INTENTIONAL

Become intentional with me.
We can be bigger than the promise, bigger than the words.
We can be more than what's been said and more than what has been heard.
Long gone are the days when we say "I want to try."
giving understanding no effort, and just say… goodbye.
With one bad move everything is gone
We lose a loving future because of stones thrown.
There is no fight or correction,
if we don't take heed and love in the right direction.
If it's not right why stand your ground,
because there will never be a second time around.

Become intentional with me.
Where your losses are my battles,
and your fears become my cares.
Indulge with me into this purpose-filled love affair.
Every opportunity becomes our reason to try.
In every situation I am by your side,
With every chance given I'll love you right.
I will do it because I want to both day and night,
intentionally loving you to make wrong things right.

So be intentional with me and don't move so fast.
To receive the love you want, you have to give love like you never have.

Impress Me!!

Impress me with your lips, Line the tip with your fingers grip, burn me with your desire, let your love get me high, then take me higher.

Let me indulge in your presence, overload on your voice and overwhelm me by your touch; overdose on you, by my own choice.

I don't want to fall in love with you... just in love-ish. I don't want to go to rehab, I ain't trying to quit.

I can be up and over you, call me what you want... just don't call unless you are calling for round two.

Three or four as we engage in acts of love making on the floor

You warm my heart with your hands as you touch my back, kiss spots on my body with your eyes, you know how I like that.

Hold me closer with every stroke, every stroke is just like dope, I need that 12 step program for love so I wont lose hope.

Some people use lines, and I do too. I just use my line to call you.

You're like my personal dope man, never say nope man. When you lay pipe, I also call you my personal plumber, man. I know you can understand what I am say'n.

I may spring a leak when I'm all alone, get my hands all wet when we talk on the phone.

I can always keep it working for a minute or two, but just in case I need something unclogged, I can always call you.

If I keep my nuts tight you will come by and make sure I did it right. If I didn't you will make sure of it tonight. Right?

Reality is…

Reality is my heart was breaking over you.
When I pride myself in loving only you,
In spite of, not because of our Indifferences and difficulties I could still rise above
and attempt to have real love.
I remain a woman of my word and love you until there's nothing left in me at all.
I tried to maintain, but ultimately it wasn't my call.
I embraced your faults and insecurities to,
I kept them all and there were a few.

Reality is it's that your "Thug" nature and the
"Church Boi" style,
You played with my emotions and I was sailing on the river called denial.
You tickled my needs and trick my thoughts,
Teased and tempted my mind... but as long as you driving,
I was riding.
I hated to see you leave, but you loved to watch me go.
I can't explain our madness, it was just something you just had to know.
Reality is my hunger was fed by your touch.
The depths of what we did was nothing more than lust.
It was longest rebound,
Maybe it wasn't love at all.
Maybe we had fallen but with the feeling of the fall.
The chase,the pursuit, the song, and the dance.
I was in love with the try and you with the chance.
The energy seemed to grow deeper and stronger.
Even though the relationship was over.
with every truth and every lie.
With every happy heart and every teary eye.

Reality is we knew from the start that this...
this would never be right.
Since the day we met all we've ever been was a fuck and a fight.
From early daylight until the wee hours of the night,
We will get it wrong, then we fight to make it right.
We can't get it together and we can no longer be friends.
Reality is…this had finally come to an end.

Sacrilegious

Close our eyes and prey on
this ride,
get down on your
knees as your imagination runs wild.
I want to sing to your glories and praise you with my cum,
gift you with my throat until this pussy wants some.
Release your demons in the depths of my thighs.
Deface and defile me...watch your demons play in my eyes.
Fill me with your Glory, let it rise up inside of me.
Chant words of ecstasy to my extremities.
Come and lay in my holy of holies, let your spirits overthrow me.
Let's not allow the good in us to prevail.
Let our passion burn a flowing fiery river from an unholy grail.
Take me to the very edge of Heaven where I can smell the stench of Hell.
Make your bed my cross and your love the nail.

We're old enough to know what comes next.
Ice in my glass, smoke in your chest.
We can set fire to the rain or just rest,
love me all over and just connect,
let's take it easy and hit reset.

Come in my bedroom and
let me lay with you.
Come let me taste you, feel you
put my body all over you.
Come let me feel you
and let me play with you
just say you want me too, feel you
put my body all over you.

The energy is high, I don't want to neglect
the chance to make the next step.
Unexpected feelings no one can explain.
deeper valleys and higher terrains
We can bottle them up or let them hang.
Conscious love making, with intentional gains.
So pick a light and let the energy feel the room.
Passion so hot it burns and consumes.

Cecyle Williams

Don't say it's too soon,
cause I'm really feeling you.
I know you want me too, feel you
put my body all over you.
Step in my bedroom,
thank me how you want to,
kiss me and squeeze me too, feel you
put my body all over you.

Say You Love Me, then Say You Love Me More

Say you love me, then say you love me more. Say you love my sense of style and you love my glowing smile. Say how you love my heart. Say how much you love our new start. Say that you love me. Baby, tell me how much you love my eyes. Say how you love the way my jeans hug my thighs. Say that you love me, and the texture of my coffee skin. Say how you love the sex, cause we're more than friends. Say that you love the kiss of my lips and the curve of my hips. Tell me you love to hear my voice, say how loving me for you is no choice.

So say that you love me, then say that you love me once more, and for you my heart will forever be an open door.

Printed in the United States
by Baker & Taylor Publisher Services